PREPARE

TO

MEET

YOUR

LORD

Formatting and Editing:
Taiwo Solomon Adeodu: +2348108673939

PREPARE TO MEET YOUR LORD

AKINBOWALE ISAAC ADEWUMI

Dedication

"And behold, I come quickly; and my reward is with me, to give every man according as his work shall be" (Revelation 22:12).

To the Sanctified in Christ.

Preface

*"Therefore, thus will I do unto thee, O Israel: and because
I will do this unto thee, prepare to meet thy God, O Israel"*
(Amos 4:12).

L ooking through the lens of human existence, there are few threads as significant, as profound and as transformative as the anticipation of meeting the Lord. Throughout history, across cultures and civilizations, the yearning for divine encounter has been a central theme, echoing in the depths of the human soul. Whether through religious devotion, spiritual seeking or existential questioning, the longing to meet one's Creator, Redeemer, or Higher Power is a universal aspect of the human experience.

Prepare to Meet Your Lord emerges as a response to this timeless longing and the pressing urgency of our present age. It is a book that seeks to address the fundamental questions of existence, the purpose of life and the ultimate destiny of the soul. It is a book that delves into the depths of spiritual wisdom, drawing from the rich tapestry of sacred texts, spiritual traditions and personal testimonies.

At its heart, "Prepare to Meet Your Lord" is a call to action, a summons to readiness and a reminder of the sacred journey that lies ahead. It is a call to prepare oneself spiritually, mentally and emotionally for the divine encounter that awaits each and every one of us. It is a call to awaken to the reality of our existence, to confront the fleeting nature of time and to embrace the eternal significance of meeting our Lord face to face. The pages of this book unfold as a tapestry of wisdom, woven together with threads of inspiration, insight and practical guidance. It is a book that explores the depths of faith, the mysteries of divine grace and the transformative power of spiritual awakening. It is a book that invites the reader on a journey of self-discovery, self-reflection and self-transformation, a journey that leads to the threshold of divine encounter.

As you embark on this journey through the pages of *Prepare to Meet Your Lord,* may you find inspiration, illumination, and transformation. May you encounter the presence of the Divine in the words you read, the thoughts you ponder and the prayers you offer. May you be guided by the wisdom of the ages, the light of divine revelation and the love of the Creator Who beckons you to Himself.

May this book serve as a guiding light on your spiritual path, a companion on your journey of preparation and a herald of the glorious day when you shall meet your Lord, face to face.

Table of Contents

1

THE NEED
FOR
PREPARATION

Introduction

IN the heart of every believer beats the anticipation of an imminent and glorious event, the return of our Lord and Saviour, Jesus Christ. This event, foretold by prophets, echoed in the teachings of Jesus Himself and affirmed throughout the New Testament, stands as the pinnacle of Christian hope and expectation. As we navigate the complexities of life in a world filled with uncertainties, preparing for the coming of the Lord becomes not only a theological concept, but a practical necessity, shaping our attitudes, actions and aspirations.

Generally, people prepare for temporary engagements such as weddings, births, school, graduations, sport tournaments, employments, journeys, retirements, funerals among other things, but they hardly prepare for life after death or the hereafter.

The purpose of this book, *Prepare to Meet Your Lord*, is to delve into the depths of this profound truth and equip believers with the knowledge, perspective and spiritual tools necessary to live in readiness for the glorious return of our King. Drawing from the rich tapestry of biblical wisdom, particularly rooted in the timeless teachings of the prophets, Christ and the apostles, we embark on a journey of exploration, revelation and transformation.

In the following chapters, we will embark on a comprehensive exploration of what it means to prepare for the coming of the Lord. We will begin by examining the signs of the times, as outlined by Jesus Himself in the gospels and discerning their relevance in the context of our modern world. From there, we will delve into the practical implications of living in readiness, cultivating a lifestyle characterized by watchfulness, prayer and faithful stewardship.

Central to our discussion will be the timeless parables and teachings of Jesus, which serve as beacons of light illuminating the path of preparation. Through the parable of the wise and foolish virgins, we will glean insights into the necessity of spiritual readiness and foresight. Likewise, we will unpack the significance of Jesus' admonition to be faithful and wise stewards of the gifts and responsibilities entrusted to us, recognizing that our preparation for His coming extends beyond mere anticipation to active engagement in His Kingdom work.

Throughout this journey, we will be guided by the profound truth that the coming of the Lord is not merely an event to be anticipated, but a reality to be lived out in our daily lives. It shapes our priorities, informs our decisions and infuses every aspect of our existence with hope and purpose. As we immerse ourselves in the study of Scripture, engage in fervent prayer and walk in faithful obedience, we position ourselves as faithful servants eagerly awaiting the arrival of our Master.

From developing a watchful mindset and cultivating a fervent life of prayer to embracing a lifestyle of faithful stewardship and service, each chapter will offer actionable insights and transformative truths to guide us on the journey of readiness.

Furthermore, this book will not only serve as a guide for personal preparation, but also as a call to action for the Body of Christ as a whole. We will examine the collective responsibility of the Church to be a beacon of light and hope in a world darkened by sin and despair, shining the light of Christ's love and truth into every corner of society.

Throughout our exploration, we will draw upon the timeless wisdom of Scripture, anchored in the King James Bible, to provide a solid foundation for our understanding and application of these principles. Whether you are a seasoned theologian, a new believer or someone exploring the Christian faith, this book is designed to meet you where you are and lead you deeper into the profound truths of God's Word.

As we embark on this journey together, may our hearts be open to receive the revelation of God's truth, our minds be sharpened by the wisdom of His Word and our spirits be ignited with a burning passion for His Kingdom. Let us prepare ourselves individually and collectively for the glorious return of our Lord and Saviour, Jesus Christ, knowing that He Who promised is faithful and His coming is sure.

With eager anticipation and steadfast faith, let us press on toward the goal of our upward call in Christ Jesus, knowing that our labour in the Lord is not in vain. May this serve as a catalyst for transformation, renewal and revival in our lives and in the Church as we prepare for the coming of the Lord and the dawn of His eternal Kingdom. May the grace and peace of God be multiplied to you as you journey through these pages and may the Holy Spirit guide you into all truth as we await the blessed hope of our salvation, the glorious appearing of our great God and Saviour, Jesus Christ.

Recognizing the Signs of the Times

"And of the children of Issachar, which were men that had understanding of the times, to know what Israel ought to do; the heads of them were two hundred; and all their brethren were at their commandment" (1 Chronicles 12:32;

14

read Luke 21:28). In the tumultuous landscape of our world today, discerning the signs of the times is akin to navigating through a dense fog with only a flickering lantern to guide our way. Yet, as believers, we are called to peer through the mist with spiritual insight, interpreting the events unfolding around us through the lens of Scripture and the guidance of the Holy Spirit. This refers to the ability to discern and understand the significant events, trends and developments occurring in the world, particularly as they relate to biblical prophecy and the overarching plan of God. This concept is rooted in various passages throughout Scripture including Matthew 16:3 and Luke 12:56 where Jesus admonishes His followers to interpret the signs of the times.

The Meaning of Signs of the Times: A prophetic sign or sign of the times is essentially a revelation or prediction concerning a historical event or technological advancement that will characterize a future period. Let's examine the First Advent of the Messiah as an illustration. The prophet Micah foretold that the Messiah would be born in the town of Bethlehem (Micah 5:2). Additionally, Daniel prophesied that the Messiah would be "cut off" 483 years after an edict was issued to rebuild Jerusalem (Daniel 9:25), with this event occurring before the destruction of the Temple in Jerusalem. Moreover, David's Psalms 22:16 mentioned the piercing of the Messiah's hands and feet. You can get more understanding of this truth from my book titled, "End Time Events."

These signs encompass various aspects, geographical, historical and technological. The birthplace of the Messiah serves as a geographical marker while the timing of His death is a historical sign. The method of execution, crucifixion, as foretold in Psalms 22, represents a technological development beyond the contemporary means of execution during David's time.

Jesus' life remarkably fulfills these prophetic signs. He was born in Bethlehem and executed in 31 AD, within the "historical window" between 27 AD and 70 AD. His crucifixion aligns with the technological prediction made centuries earlier. The fulfillment of these signs in Jesus' life serves to validate His identity as the prophesied Messiah.

Although there are over 300 prophecies in the Hebrew Scriptures about the First Coming of the Messiah, many are repetitive. For instance, the Messiah's lineage from the house of David is reiterated several times. Upon eliminating these repetitions, there remain 109 distinct prophecies that find fulfillment in Jesus' life.

These Messianic signs underscore the meticulous orchestration of God's plan throughout history and affirm the authenticity of Jesus as the fulfillment of ancient prophecies. They serve as compelling evidence of God's faithfulness and His sovereign control over the unfolding of events.

The Messianic Signs: In the teachings of Jesus, a poignant moment occurred when the Pharisees and Sadducees approached Him, demanding a "sign" to prove His Messiahship. *"The Pharisees also with the Sadducees came, and tempting desired him that he would shew them a sign from heaven. He answered and said unto them, when it is evening, ye say, It will be fair weather: for the sky is red. And in the morning, It will be foul weather to day: for the sky is red and lowering. O ye hypocrites, ye can discern the face of the sky; but can ye not discern the signs of the times? A wicked and adulterous generation seeketh after a sign; and there shall no sign be given unto it, but the sign of the prophet Jonas. And he left them and departed"* (Matthew 16:1-4).

Their expectation was a miraculous display. However, Jesus redirected their focus, urging them to discern the signs of the times rather than seeking a mere miracle. He employed the term "sign" to allude to the fulfilled prophecies in His life, emphasizing their significance in recognizing His identity. Similarly, the Second Coming of Jesus is punctuated with prophetic signs, woven throughout the Old and New Testaments.

Over 500 prophecies in the Old Testament and frequent references in the New Testament underscore this momentous event. These prophecies serve as guideposts, signaling the approach of the Lord's return. Jesus himself underscored the importance of recognizing these signs in His Olivet discourse. He delineated a catalogue of signs indicative of the end times, culminating with the directive to discern their significance, for his return would be imminent (Matthew 24:33). Paul echoed this sentiment in his letters, assuring believers that though the Lord's return might appear sudden to the world, those who walk in the light are granted insight into the signs of the times by the indwelling presence of the Holy Spirit (1 Thessalonians 5:1-6).

Furthermore, the author of Hebrews exhorts believers to encourage one another as they witness the approaching day of judgment (Hebrews 10:25). Thus, the recognition of prophetic signs serves, not only as a testament to the faithfulness of God's Word, but also as a call to readiness and vigilance among believers.

In essence, these Messianic signs beckon believers to cultivate spiritual discernment and attentiveness to the unfolding of God's divine plan, ensuring that they are not caught unawares by the imminent return of the Lord.

Signs of the End Times: The re-establishment of the nation of Israel stands as a profound historical sign of the end times. Throughout the Hebrew Scriptures, prophecies repeatedly foretell the restoration of Israel before the return of the Messiah (Isaiah 11:10-12; Ezekiel 37:1-12; Amos 9:13-15; Zechariah 12:1-3). Jesus himself emphasized this sign in Matthew 24, likening it to the budding of a fig tree, symbolizing Israel's revival. He declared that the generation witnessing this event would not pass away before His return (Matthew 24:34).

Likewise, the book of Revelation unveils numerous technological signs pertaining to the end times. For instance, it prophesies unprecedented devastation during the first three and a half years of the Tribulation, with one-half of the world's population perishing (Revelation 6-9). Such extensive carnage suggests the utilization of advanced weaponry, possibly indicating the development of nuclear weapons and their delivery systems.

Another prophecy in Revelation describes a scenario where the entire world beholds the bodies of the two witnesses for three and a half days after their death (Revelation 11:9). This seemingly improbable event finds plausibility through modern technology like television and satellite transmission.

Moreover, Revelation prophesies the emergence of a massive army of 200 million soldiers from Asia marching towards Israel during the Tribulation period. Given the world's population at the time of the prophecy's writing, the notion seemed inconceivable. However, with the exponential growth in global population, especially in regions like China, this prophecy becomes increasingly feasible in the modern era.

These signs serve as veritable reminders of the intricate interplay between biblical prophecy and historical developments. They prompt believers to discern the signs of the times, fostering a heightened awareness of the imminence of Christ's return and the fulfillment of God's redemptive plan.

In contemplating the signs of the last days as foretold in Scripture, it becomes evident that we are indeed living in a pivotal era of earth's history. II Peter 3:3-4 warns of scoffers who will mock the truth and deny the promised return of Jesus, a skepticism that has pervaded throughout time. Yet, amidst the chaos and uncertainty, spiritual insight reveals that these signs are not merely coincidental, but rather indicative of a greater divine plan unfolding.

The prevalence of wars and conflicts, as stated in Mark 13:7-8, serves as a tangible manifestation of the unrest that characterizes this age. Such turmoil is echoed in Matthew 24:14 where the necessity for the gospel to be proclaimed to all nations before the end can come is emphasized. However, this proclamation is not without opposition, for false prophets and deceptive figures, as warned in Matthew 24:23-24, seek to lead astray even the faithful.

Moreover, the cosmic signs described in Matthew 24:29-30 illustrate the cosmic upheaval that will accompany the culmination of this age, prompting reflection on the moral decay prevalent in society, as outlined in II Timothy 3:1-5. This moral decline is mirrored by the pursuit of self-interest and pleasure at the expense of spiritual values.

In the midst of these tumultuous signs, individuals are called to maintain vigilance and spiritual readiness as articulated in Matthew 24:42-44. The anticipation of Christ's return necessitates a steadfast commitment to faith and righteousness, even amidst the allure of peace and security, as cautioned in I Thessalonians 5:2-3.

In General, human life, likened to morning flowers, blooms with vitality and fragrance, yet eventually succumbs to the inevitable sunset where even the brightest glimmer fades into gloom. The veil of ignorance that shrouds humanity often obscures the clarity of what lies ahead and how it will unfold. However, unlike mortals, God transcends time and comprehends every beginning and ending, from the last fleeting moments of individuals to the distant horizons of a millennium yet to unfold.

This profound truth should draw us nearer to God, the omniscient Architect Who orchestrates the tapestry of existence. We are compelled to live in readiness for the imminent, having repented of our transgressions and reconciled with our Creator. Such urgency echoes the central theme of Christ's gospel which beckons us to embrace salvation without compromise. Imagine the profound impact of sharing this saving truth with someone on the brink of perishing, unaware of their impending fate. Such a soul may experience the transformative grace exemplified by the repentant thief who found redemption beside the Saviour on the cross.

When we immerse ourselves in the gospel of Jesus Christ, we gain insight into the signs of the times, discerning the currents of divine providence amidst the ebb and flow of human history. In contrast to the ignorance that befell the ancient Israelites, contemporary believers must shun such fatal unawareness. By embracing the gospel's illumination, we navigate the complexities of our era with clarity and purpose, equipped to discern the signs of the day and respond with faithfulness and vigilance. Consider the global geopolitical landscape where tensions simmer and conflicts brew.

Spiritual insight prompts us to recognize these geopolitical shifts as indicators of the times, aligning with the prophetic warnings of Scripture. However, amidst the darkness, there are beacons of light. 1 Chronicles 12:32 commends the sons of Issachar for their understanding of the times and their ability to discern what Israel ought to do.

Similarly, in our modern era, believers are called to emulate the wisdom of the sons of Issachar, diligently studying the Word of God and seeking divine guidance to navigate the complexities of our world. Consequently, the signs of the last days serve not as harbingers of despair, but as reminders of the imminence of God's ultimate redemption. As such, it is incumbent upon believers to heed the admonitions of Scripture, anchoring themselves in faith and spiritual discernment as they navigate the tumult of these unprecedented times.

1.0 Understanding the Signs of Christ's Imminent Return

In Revelation 1:7-8, *"Behold, he cometh with clouds; and every eye shall see him, and they also which pierced him: and all kindreds of the earth shall wail because of him. Even so, Amen. I am Alpha and Omega, the beginning and the ending, saith the Lord, which is, and which was, and which is to come, the Almighty."*

Alpha and Omega are symbolic representations of Christ's eternal nature and divine authority. As the Alpha, He is the beginning of all things, while as the Omega, He is the end and culmination of all things. This imagery highlights Christ's sovereignty over time, history and eternity. He encompasses all the qualities, attributes and perfections of the Almighty God, establishing His deity unequivocally.

Revelation 22:14-16 says, *"Blessed are they that do his commandments, that they may have right to the tree of life and may enter in through the gates into the city. For without are dogs, and sorcerers, and whoremongers, and murderers, and idolaters, and whosoever loveth and maketh a lie. I Jesus have sent mine angel to testify unto you these things in the churches. I am the root and the offspring of David, and the bright and morning star."*

In furtherance, Christ's identification as the "root and offspring of David" underscores His pre-eminence and eternal existence. Just as a tree grows from its root before sprouting, Christ existed before David and before all creation. He came as the first Adam lost fellowship with God in Eden, seeking to reconcile humanity to its Creator and restore the privileges lost in the first paradise.

The anticipation of Christ's imminent return permeates the entirety of Scripture, emphasizing its certainty and significance. This expectation serves as a beacon of hope for believers and a call to repentance for sinners. Though some may question or delay in acknowledging this truth, the delay in Christ's return is a gracious opportunity for believers to propagate the gospel and for sinners to repent and be saved.

In the heavenly paradise, symbolized by the pure river of water of life flowing from the throne of God and the Lamb, there will be uninterrupted light and eternal sustenance for the saints. The tree of life, nourished by the life-giving river, bears twelve kinds of fruit, providing perpetual health and happiness to God's redeemed.

With the eradication of pain, curse, tears and death, the saints will reign with the King of kings eternally, fulfilling

God's eternal purpose of establishing a Kingdom of kings and priests.

Every prophecy concerning Christ's first coming was fulfilled literally and likewise, those pertaining to His second coming will be fulfilled without fail. The anticipation of His return is woven throughout Scripture with numerous references emphasizing its importance and inevitability. As believers eagerly await His coming, let us remain steadfast in faith, serving Him faithfully and rejoicing in the promise of eternal fellowship with our Redeemer.

The concept of the rapture preceding Christ's second coming is a widely held belief among Christians, distinguishing the two events by a span of seven years. Unlike the second coming, which will be visible to all, the rapture is a moment when only the saints will see Christ, as He appears in the sky to gather them to Himself. At His second coming, however, Christ will return to the earth visibly to live and reign for one thousand years with the saints. Additionally, while Christ comes for the saints at the rapture, He will come with the raptured saints at His second coming.

The imminence of the rapture underscores the urgency for readiness and repentance. Prophecies serve as warnings and calls to prepare for these imminent events. Those who persist in wrongdoing despite hearing the truth will seal their fate in hell, while those who continue in righteousness demonstrate their saving faith and secure their place in heaven.

Preliminary Signs of Christ's Return
False Messiahs: Individuals and groups claiming to be messiahs or Saviours, deceiving many with false teachings and doctrines.
Wars and Rumours of Wars: The prevalence of conflicts and unrest among nations, resulting in fear, death and suffering.
Natural Calamities: Increasing occurrences of famines, pestilences, earthquakes and other natural disasters, causing devastation and testing faith in God.
Persecution: Intensified persecution of Christians throughout history, with the twentieth century witnessing unprecedented levels of martyrdom and suffering.
Apostasy: A gradual departure from the faith and rejection of biblical truths, accompanied by a decline in moral standards and spiritual fervour.
Cynicism: A prevailing attitude of indifference and skepticism towards spiritual matters, fueled by increasing wickedness and false teachings.

Primary Signs of Christ's Return
Preaching of the Gospel: The proclamation of the gospel of the Kingdom to all nations, indicating the nearing culmination of God's redemptive plan.

Abomination of Desolation: A period of unparalleled tribulation marked by widespread devastation and terror, prompting believers to flee and seek refuge.

Sign of the Son: A supernatural sign heralding the imminent return of Jesus, characterized by His appearance in the clouds with power and glory, accompanied by mourning and recognition of His divine identity.

These signs serve as indicators of the approaching end of the age and the fulfillment of biblical prophecy. While some have already occurred throughout history, others are yet to be fulfilled, underscoring the need for vigilance, discernment and faithful adherence to God's Word as we await the glorious return of our Lord and Saviour, Jesus Christ.

The Precise Time of Christ's Return

No One Knows: Jesus emphasizes that the exact day and hour of His Second Advent are known only to the Father, cautioning against attempts to set specific dates. While angels and Jesus Himself, in His human capacity, are unaware of the timing, those familiar with prophecy may discern the approximate time based on certain events, such as the Abomination of Desolation.

Like the Days of Noah: Jesus compares His coming to the days of Noah, not due to the wickedness of that time, but because people were unaware of the impending judgment despite Noah's warnings. When the flood came and Noah entered the ark, it was too late for those who had ignored the message.

The Principles Sign of Christ's Return

The Rapture of the Church: While not explicitly mentioned in the Olivet Discourse, the concept of the rapture is inferred from verses such as Matthew 24:40-41. The rapture involves the removal of believers (the Church) from the earth to meet the Lord in the air, preceding the final period of earth's history.

Scriptures such as 1 Thessalonians 4:15-18 and 1 Corinthians 15:51-52 describe this event, where believers will be caught up to be with the Lord forever, experiencing a transformation from mortal to immortal. Jesus exhorts believers to remain vigilant and watchful, emphasizing the uncertainty of the timing of His return and the importance of readiness.

The Preparation for Christ's Return

Despite the sobering nature of prophecy, there are rays of comfort and hope. The hour of God's grace has not yet expired, providing an opportunity for salvation and reconciliation. The focal point of many prophecies is Israel and certain events involving Israel, such as peace and the rebuilding of the temple, must occur before the end times unfold fully.

Jesus' promise of preparing a place for believers in His Father's house offers comfort amidst uncertainty, reminding us of His sovereign control over history and his ultimate victory over darkness.

As believers face the future with anticipation and faith, they find assurance in God's promises and the certainty of His plan unfolding according to His divine will. Despite the challenges and tribulations ahead, the hope of Christ's return shines brightly, illuminating the path to eternal joy and fulfillment.

1.1 Interpreting Current Events in Light of Biblical Prophecy

In 2 Timothy 3:1-8, it sets the stage for understanding that the period preceding the return of Christ will be marked by challenging and perilous times. The moral and ethical decline that will characterize society in the last days. People prioritize self-interest, wealth and personal ambition over virtues like humility, gratitude and holiness.

The societal decay, including a lack of empathy, a propensity for violence, a disregard for what is morally right and good and the prioritizing of worldly pleasures over genuine devotion to God is prevalent. In view of this, the Scripture serves as a warning to maintain spiritual discernment and integrity in the face of societal corruption.

Interpreting current events in the world in the light of biblical prophecy would require a practice undertaken by many believers who seek to understand how contemporary developments align with or fulfill predictions found in the Bible. Here are some common approaches and considerations:

Study of End Times Prophecy: Many Christians focus on passages in the Bible, particularly in books like Daniel, Ezekiel, Matthew (specifically chapters 24 and 25) and Revelation, that are believed to contain prophecies about the end times. They examine world events through the lens of these prophecies to discern if current events align with what is predicted. Matthew 24 chapter contains Jesus' Olivet Discourse, where he speaks about signs of the end times, including wars, famines, earthquakes and false prophets. While the entire book of Revelation provides vivid imagery and symbolic language about the end times and the rise of a global government, persecution of believers and the return of Christ.

Israel and the Middle East: Given the significance of Israel in biblical prophecy, events in the Middle East, especially those involving Israel and its neighbours, often receive close attention. This includes developments related to the peace process, conflicts and geopolitical shifts in the region.

Technology and Globalization: Some interpretations of biblical prophecy suggest that advancements in technology and globalization are paving the way for the fulfillment of certain end-time scenarios such as a one-world government or the implementation of a global surveillance system. *"But thou, O Daniel, shut up the words, and seal the book, even to the time of the end: many shall run to and fro, and knowledge shall be increased"* (Daniel 12:4). Also, the mark of the beast is often interpreted in modern contexts as a form of global identification or surveillance system (Revelation 13:16-18).

Natural Disasters and Environmental Concerns: The increase in natural disasters and environmental degradation such as earthquakes, glacial melting, flood, outbreak of fire, are sometimes interpreted as fulfilling passages in the Bible that speak of "birth pains" or signs of the end times. This perspective sees these events as indicators of the earth's groaning and the imminent return of Christ. In Matthew 24:7, Jesus speaks of "famines and earthquakes in various places" as signs of the end times.

Moral and Social Trends: Many Christians interpret societal shifts such as increasing secularization, moral decay and the erosion of traditional values as fulfilling biblical warnings about the last days. They may see parallels between these trends and passages that describe widespread lawlessness and spiritual apostasy. 2 Timothy 3:1-5 describes a list of moral decay and societal traits that would characterize the last days. Isaiah 5:20: *"Woe to those who call evil good and good evil, who put darkness for light and light for darkness."*

Global Events and International Relations: Significant global events, such as conflicts, economic crises, famine, wars, and pandemics, are often scrutinized for their potential relevance to biblical prophecy. Some believers see these events as evidence of the world's instability and the fulfillment of prophetic warnings about the end times. Ezekiel 38-39 harped on prophecies about a future invasion of Israel by a coalition of nations, which some interpret as modern-day geopolitical alliances. In Daniel 2, the vision of the statue representing successive world empires culminates in a final kingdom represented by feet of iron and clay.

Cultural and Religious Developments: Changes in religious demographics, the rise of secularism and shifts in cultural norms are interpreted through the prism of biblical prophecy especially regarding predictions about the rise of false religions and the persecution of believers. 2 Thessalonians 2:3-4 mentions a "falling away" or apostasy before the revealing of the "man of lawlessness" who sets himself up as God. Likewise, Revelation 13 describes a beast rising out of the sea with blasphemous names and the worship of the dragon (Satan).

It is important to note that interpretations of current events in the light of biblical prophecy can vary widely among Christians and different theological perspectives may lead to divergent understandings of the significance of specific events.

Additionally, caution should be exercised to avoid dogmatic assertions about the timing or specifics of prophetic fulfillment because interpretations are often speculative and subject to debate.

The needful has to be done: *"And in the morning, it will be foul weather to day: for the sky is red and lowering. O ye hypocrites, ye can discern the face of the sky; but can ye not discern the signs of the times? And he called his ten servants, and delivered them ten pounds, and said unto them, Occupy till I come"* (Matthew 16:3; Luke 19:13).

The passage emphasizes the importance of maintaining a balanced perspective on interpreting current events in the light of biblical prophecy. Here's a breakdown of the key points:

Humility and Perspective: While there may be disagreements among good people about the specifics of prophetic fulfillment, it's important to maintain humility and recognize that ultimately, God is in control and His will shall prevail.

Attention to Current Events: Although we should not obsess over every detail or attempt to predict the exact timing of Christ's return, we are called to observe the times and be alert for signs of the end times.

Unchanging Truths from Scripture: Despite the ever-changing nature of headlines and events, there are foundational truths from Scripture that remain constant:

- God is sovereign and His will is paramount.
- Christ will return again.
- God is not bound by time and what may seem like delay is part of His divine plan.
- We should avoid trying to predict the timing of Christ's return.
- We are called to maintain a balance between watchful expectation and diligent labour in the service of God.

2. **Diligent Labour and Faithful Living**: In light of the certainty of Christ's return, believers are called to engage in various activities:
   - Evangelizing and discipling the lost.
   - Edifying fellow believers.
   - Caring for our families.
   - Striving for personal spiritual growth and Christlikeness.
   - Glorifying God in all aspects of life.

3. **Occupying Till He Comes**: The phrase "occupy till He comes" underscores the idea that while we await Christ's return, we are to be actively engaged in fulfilling God's purposes on earth. This involves faithfully carrying out the tasks and responsibilities assigned to us as followers of Christ.

Overall, the passage encourages believers to maintain a balanced perspective, grounded in the unchanging truths of Scripture, while actively participating in God's work until the return of Christ.

1.2   The Biblical Prophecies of the Second Coming

During the ascension of Jesus, two men clothed in white appeared to the disciples, prompting them to cease their gaze into the sky. These celestial messengers conveyed a profound message, affirming that the same Jesus who ascended into heaven would return in a tangible form. This episode, chronicled in Acts 1:11, serves as a pivotal moment, emphasizing the corporeal nature of Christ's eventual return.

The anticipation of Christ's second coming is woven intricately throughout biblical prophecy, with an astonishing 1 in every 25 verses in the New Testament referencing this event. These prophecies underscore the significance of Jesus' return, symbolizing the culmination of divine promises and the fulfillment of God's plan for humanity.

In John 14:2-3, Jesus himself foretold his return, reassuring His disciples with the promise of preparation and reunion. He speaks of His Father's house, abundant with rooms awaiting their arrival. This assurance not only speaks to the tangible reality of Christ's return, but also conveys the intimacy of His relationship with His followers, promising to personally escort them to their eternal dwelling place.

Thus, through the convergence of biblical accounts and Christ's own words, we are reminded of the certainty and significance of His return. It is not merely a spiritual event, but a tangible manifestation of divine promise, heralding the ultimate fulfillment of God's redemptive plan for humanity.

Moreover, the Bible contains numerous prophecies concerning the Second Coming of Jesus Christ, offering believers a glimpse into the future and instilling hope in the fulfillment of God's promises. Here are some key biblical prophecies related to the Second Coming:

Jesus' Own Predictions: In the Olivet Discourse (Matthew 24, Mark 13, Luke 21), Jesus Himself foretold signs that would precede His return. These include wars, famines, earthquakes, persecution of believers, the preaching of the gospel to all nations, the abomination of desolation and cosmic signs such as the darkening of the sun and moon.

The Return in Glory: Revelation 19:11-16 describes Jesus' return in glory, riding on a white horse with the armies of heaven following Him. He is depicted as the conquering King, defeating His enemies and establishing His Kingdom on earth.

The Resurrection of Believers: 1 Thessalonians 4:16-17 speaks of the resurrection of believers at the Second Coming of Christ. The dead in Christ will rise first, followed by those who are alive and remain, who will be caught up together with them to meet the Lord in the air.

The Judgment of the Nations: In Matthew 25:31-46, Jesus describes the judgment of the nations that will occur at His Second Coming. He will separate the righteous from the wicked, rewarding the righteous with eternal life and condemning the wicked to eternal punishment.

The Restoration of Israel: Many prophecies in the Old Testament, such as Ezekiel 36-37 and Zechariah 12-14, speak of the restoration and blessing of Israel in the last days. The Second Coming of Christ will usher in a time of spiritual renewal and fulfillment of God's promises to His chosen people.

The Millennial Reign: Revelation 20:1-6 describes a thousand-year period (the millennium) during which Christ will reign on earth with His saints. Satan will be bound, and there will be peace and righteousness throughout the earth.

The New Heaven and New Earth: Revelation 21-22 presents a vision of the new heaven and new earth, where God will dwell with His people for eternity. There will be no more death, sorrow, or pain, and God will make all things new.

These prophecies provide believers with assurance that God's plans for the future are certain and that His promises will be fulfilled.

They also serve as a reminder to live in readiness, eagerly awaiting the glorious return of Jesus Christ and the establishment of His eternal Kingdom.

2

LIVING IN
READINESS
AT ALL TIMES

THE final section of the article underscores the contemporary relevance of the second coming of Christ, drawing a parallel between the scoffers described in 2 Peter 3 and the skeptics of today who question the significance of Jesus' return and the teachings of the Bible regarding this event. Just as the scoffers of old mockingly asked, "Where is this 'coming' He promised?" So too do many in today's world prioritize self-indulgence and material possessions over matters of the spirit.

The attitudes and actions prevalent in today's society serve to deny Christ, just as they did in Peter's time. The teachings of Jesus are frequently undermined and contradicted, posing a significant challenge to the faith of believers. In a world where temptations and pressures abound, it is all too easy to succumb to the example set by the scoffers and lead a life of denial of Christ and His teachings.

However, the passage from Titus 2:12-13 provides a clear directive for Christians: to reject ungodliness and worldly lusts while eagerly anticipating the blessed hope of Christ's return. Being prepared for the second coming involves actively resisting the attitudes and behaviours of the world and striving to emulate Christ in every aspect of life. By doing so, believers ensure that when Christ does return, they will be acknowledged as those who remained steadfast and true to Him.

In essence, being prepared for the second coming requires a deliberate choice to prioritize spiritual matters over worldly concerns, to reject the influences of a skeptical and materialistic culture and to faithfully follow the teachings of Christ. Only by remaining vigilant and steadfast in our faith can we hope to be found worthy of acknowledgment by our great God and Saviour Jesus Christ upon His glorious return.

In 2 Timothy 2:3-4; Apostle Paul writes: *"Thou therefore endure hardness, as a good soldier of Jesus Christ. No man that warreth entangleth himself with the affairs of this life; that he may please him who hath chosen him to be a soldier."* Living in readiness for Christ's return involves enduring hardships and avoiding entanglement in worldly affairs. Just as a soldier focuses on pleasing their commanding officer, believers should prioritize pleasing God in their lives.

In view of this, believers are encouraged to diligently confirm their calling and election by living out their faith. This involves being grounded in God's Word, allowing it to shape and mould us into mature disciples of Christ. Scripture provides the guidance and wisdom necessary for living a life that pleases God by actively pursuing spiritual growth and obedience to God's commands. By doing so, believers can have confidence in their salvation and readiness for Christ's return.

In every moment, whether consciously acknowledged or not, each of us is embroiled in a spiritual battle. This profound truth should lead us, as instructed in Scripture, to live with spiritual sobriety, not with joyless spirits, but with joy, hope and peace, all while mindful of the constant confrontation with a relentless and formidable adversary who seeks our distraction and destruction.

This adversary is one before whom earthly powers pale in comparison, a foe against whom even the mightiest rulers, commanders, armies or nations would tremble and despair. Our hope, therefore, does not reside in human strength, but in the profound reality of the life, death and resurrection of our Saviour and Lord Jesus Christ.

Through His sacrificial death, Jesus has provided us with the means to break free from the grip of the Destroyer and to be welcomed joyfully into the family of God, those who have placed their unwavering faith in Jesus Christ alone and endeavour to follow His guidance in their lives.

Every member of God's family is enlisted in this global spiritual warfare. Just as Paul urged Timothy, so too are we called to endure hardship as faithful soldiers of Christ Jesus, untangled from the distractions of everyday life, striving to please the One Who has called us into His service.

Just as no soldier would venture into battle unprepared, so too must we ensure that we and our fellow soldiers are equipped with the training and tools necessary for victory. This underscores the significance of Paul's teaching in 2 Timothy 3:17, where he emphasizes the transformative power of God's Word, which equips us for every good work as we submit ourselves to its teachings.

In 2 Peter 1:10-11, Peter writes: *"Wherefore the rather, brethren, give diligence to make your calling and election sure: for if ye do these things, ye shall never fall: For so an entrance shall be ministered unto you abundantly into the everlasting kingdom of our Lord and Saviour Jesus Christ."* This called for a steadfast commitment to spiritual growth, moral integrity and unwavering faithfulness to the calling we have received in Christ. Hence, Peter urges believers to "give diligence" to make their "calling and election sure." This implies an active and intentional effort to confirm and solidify one's relationship with God. It involves seeking God earnestly through prayer, studying His Word diligently and aligning one's life with His will. By doing so, believers can have assurance of their salvation and stand firm in their faith, rooted in the truth of God's promises.

Secondly, Peter emphasizes the importance of "doing these things" as a means to avoid stumbling or falling away from the faith. This underscores the need for consistent obedience and perseverance in the Christian walk. By continually practicing righteousness, pursuing holiness and resisting temptation, believers can maintain their spiritual vitality and remain steadfast in their commitment to Christ.

Finally, Peter assures believers that by living in readiness and faithfully fulfilling their calling, they will receive an abundant entrance into the everlasting Kingdom of our Lord and Saviour Jesus Christ. This highlights the ultimate reward awaiting those who remain faithful to the end, the glorious inheritance of eternal life in the presence of God.

As God equips us, we become proficient warriors, adept at utilizing the weapons He has provided for this spiritual warfare. Our readiness for battle is directly correlated with our growth in understanding and obedience to His Word. Therefore, we must redouble our commitment to immerse ourselves in Scripture, praying, discussing and applying its truths to every facet of our lives. Confident in the victory that is ours through Christ and living in accordance with

God's will, believers can confidently look forward to the day when they will enter into the fullness of God's Kingdom for all eternity.

In summary, living in readiness for Christ's return entails enduring hardships, avoiding entanglement in worldly affairs, confirming our calling and election through diligent pursuit of faith and being thoroughly equipped by Scripture for every good work. It is a life of dedication, obedience and spiritual growth, motivated by the anticipation of Christ's imminent return.

2.1 The Importance of Being Prepared

Preparation is not merely a practical necessity; it is a spiritual imperative that permeates every aspect of life. Whether we are preparing for an exam, a job interview, a journey or the coming of the Lord, readiness is paramount. Here are several reasons why being prepared holds immense significance:

Spiritual Readiness: As believers, we are called to be spiritually prepared for the coming of the Lord. Jesus Himself emphasized the importance of watchfulness and readiness, urging His disciples to be prepared for His return at any moment (Matthew 24:42-44). Spiritual preparation involves cultivating a deep relationship with God, living a life of faith and obedience and being vigilant in prayer and service.

Opportunity Recognition: Being prepared enables us to recognize and seize opportunities when they arise. Whether in our personal, professional or spiritual lives, readiness positions us to make the most of favourable circumstances and respond effectively to challenges.

Peace of Mind: Preparedness brings a sense of peace and confidence, knowing that we have done everything within our power to face whatever may come our way. By anticipating potential obstacles and having a plan in place, we can navigate through life's uncertainties with greater assurance and resilience.

Efficiency and Effectiveness: Preparation enhances our efficiency and effectiveness in achieving our goals. By investing time and effort in planning and organization, we can streamline our efforts, minimize distractions and maximize productivity.

Resilience in Times of Crisis: Preparedness equips us to withstand and overcome unexpected crises and hardships. Whether it is a natural disaster, a health emergency or a personal setback, having a contingency plan in place enables us to respond calmly and decisively, minimizing the impact of adverse circumstances.

Personal Growth and Development: The process of preparation fosters personal growth and development. It requires discipline, perseverance and a willingness to step out of our comfort zones. Through preparation, we hone our skills, expand our knowledge and cultivate the resilience needed to face life's challenges.

Fulfillment of Purpose: Being prepared positions us to fulfill our God-given purpose and destiny. Whether it's fulfilling a specific calling, achieving professional success or making a positive impact in our communities, readiness enables us to step into our divine assignments with confidence and clarity.

In essence, being prepared is not just about anticipating future events; it is about embracing a mindset of readiness that permeates every aspect of our lives. By prioritizing spiritual preparedness, seizing opportunities, maintaining peace of mind, enhancing efficiency, building resilience, fostering personal growth and fulfilling our purpose, we can navigate through life with confidence, purpose and effectiveness.

2.2   The Promise of Eternal Life

The promise of eternal life is a central theme throughout the Bible, offering hope and assurance to believers of all ages. This promise encompasses, not only the continuation of life beyond physical death, but also the fullness of life in fellowship with God for eternity. Acknowledging the weight of prophecies leading to the climactic event of the Second Coming, Christians are deeply aware of its eminent significance.

Throughout centuries, since the initial promise of Christ's return, believers have held diverse interpretations regarding the doctrine and the associated events. However, irrespective of differing perspectives on the Second Advent, a Christian's life should be characterized by a transcendent hope that anticipates an eternity in the presence of God.

This enduring truth has sustained believers across generations during times of trial and persecution. It serves as a timeless message, urging Christians of every era to pursue godliness while resisting the allure of worldliness. Central to this message is the glorious promise of life in the age to come.

Jesus Himself emphasized this promise in John 14:1-3, offering it as solace to His disciples amidst the upheaval of imminent events. This assurance of eternal life was intended to bolster believers throughout their own trials and persecutions.

In the book of Titus, Paul refers to this promise as the "blessed hope, even the appearing of the glory of our great God and Saviour Jesus Christ" (Titus 2:13). The appearing and revelation of Jesus Christ in human history mark the end of the present age and the beginning of the age to come. In this new era, God's reign will be fully realized in the New Heavens and New Earth, where justice and righteousness will prevail.

The appearing of Jesus Christ holds profound significance for believers as it brings the fulfillment of their hope in the promise of eternal life. It heralds the culmination of God's redemptive plan wherein believers will dwell in His presence for eternity, experiencing the fullness of His glory and love. Here are some key aspects of the promise of eternal life as revealed in Scripture:

God's Gift: Eternal life is described as a gift from God (Romans 6:23). It is not something that can be earned or achieved through human effort, but is freely given to those who believe in Jesus Christ as their Saviour.

Through Jesus Christ: Jesus Himself proclaimed, *"I am the way, the truth, and the life. No one comes to the Father except through me"* (John 14:6). He is the Source and Mediator of eternal life and through faith in Him, believers receive the gift of salvation and eternal life (John 3:16).

Spiritual Rebirth: Jesus taught that in order to inherit eternal life, one must be born again spiritually (John 3:3-5). This spiritual rebirth occurs through faith in Christ and the indwelling of the Holy Spirit Who seals believers for the day of redemption (Ephesians 1:13-14).

Resurrection: The promise of eternal life includes the resurrection of the body. Just as Jesus was raised from the dead, so too will believers experience resurrection to eternal life (1 Corinthians 15:20-23). This resurrection will occur at the return of Christ when the dead in Christ will be raised imperishable and the living believers will be transformed (1 Thessalonians 4:16-17).

Quality of Life: Eternal life is not merely an endless duration of existence, but also a quality of life characterized by intimacy with God, joy, peace and fulfillment. Jesus described it as "abundant life" (John 10:10) and promised that those who believe in Him will never thirst or hunger spiritually (John 6:35).

Freedom from Death: The promise of eternal life includes freedom from the power and fear of death. Jesus declared, *"I am the resurrection and the life. He who believes in me, though he may die, he shall live"* (John 11:25). Believers can face death with confidence, knowing that it is not the end, but the gateway to eternal life with God.

Everlasting Fellowship with God: The ultimate fulfillment of the promise of eternal life is eternal fellowship with God in His presence. Revelation 21:3-4 describes the New Heaven and New Earth, where God will dwell with His people and they will be His children and He will wipe away every tear from their eyes.

In conclusion, the promise of eternal life is a foundational truth of the Christian faith, rooted in the person and work of Jesus Christ. It is a gift of God's grace, received through faith and it encompasses spiritual rebirth, resurrection, abundant life, freedom from death and everlasting fellowship with God. This promise gives believers hope and assurance in the midst of life's trials and uncertainties, knowing that their ultimate destiny is secure in Christ for eternity.

3

PRACTICAL STEPS TO PREPARE FOR THE COMING OF THE LORD

DEEPENING one's relationship with God through prayer and worship is crucial for spiritual survival. In Matthew 26:41 and other Scriptures, the importance of watching and praying is emphasized as a means to escape the corruption in the world caused by evil desires (1 Peter 1:4) and to remain alert at all times.

It is often said that one's state in times of crisis will reflect the depth of their prayer and worship life. If we neglect prayer and worship, we are essentially declaring our self-sufficiency and lack of need for God's guidance, comfort or strength. This stems from pride and self-deception, indicating weakened faith in God's character and promises. In such times, we may rely on human wisdom or succumb to fleshly desires.

51

Prioritizing prayer and worship demonstrate our dependence on God and our recognition of His sovereignty. By consistently approaching the throne of grace, we cultivate spiritual poise and confidence in our access to God's power and His ability to work in and through us.

Preparing for the coming of the Lord is not just a theoretical concept, but a practical lifestyle that believers are called to embrace. Here are some practical steps to help prepare for the coming of the Lord:

Seek a Deeper Relationship with God: Cultivate a daily habit of prayer, Bible study and meditation to grow closer to God. Develop a personal relationship with Jesus Christ and allow the Holy Spirit to transform your heart and mind.

Repentance and Confession of Sin: Regularly examine your heart and confess any sins to God. Repentance is essential for spiritual renewal and preparation for the Lord's coming (1 John 1:9).

Live a Life of Holiness and Purity: Strive to live a life of holiness and purity, honouring God in your thoughts, words and actions. Avoid sin and temptation and pursue righteousness and godliness (1 Thessalonians 4:7).

Be Watchful and Alert: Stay vigilant and alert to the signs of the times as Jesus instructed His disciples (Matthew 24:42). Pay attention to current events in light of biblical prophecy, but do not be consumed by fear or speculation.

Share the Gospel: Be a witness for Christ by sharing the good news of salvation with others. Live out your faith in word and deed, demonstrating the love and compassion of Jesus to those around you (Matthew 28:19-20).

Serve Others in Love: Look for opportunities to serve others in love, following the example of Jesus Who came not to be served, but to serve (Matthew 20:28). Practice kindness, generosity and compassion toward those in need.

Forgive Others: Extend forgiveness to those who have wronged you, as Christ has forgiven you (Colossians 3:13). Let go of bitterness, resentment and grudges and seek reconciliation and restoration in relationships.

Be Prepared Spiritually and Practically: While we anticipate the Lord's return, we must also be prepared for the uncertainties of life. This includes being spiritually grounded, but also being responsible stewards of our resources, planning for the future and caring for our families and communities.

Pray for His Coming: Pray earnestly for the Lord's return, echoing the words of the early church, "Even so, come, Lord Jesus!" (Revelation 22:20). Pray for His Kingdom to come and His will to be done on earth as it is in heaven (Matthew 6:10).

Remain Faithful and Endure: Finally, persevere in faithfulness and endurance, knowing that our labour in the Lord is not in vain (1 Corinthians 15:58). Stay grounded in the truth of God's Word and hold fast to the hope of His promised return.

In conclusion, preparing for the coming of the Lord involves both spiritual and practical steps. By seeking a deeper relationship with God, living a life of holiness and purity, being watchful and alert, sharing the gospel, serving others in love, forgiving others, being prepared spiritually and practically, praying for His coming and remaining faithful and enduring, believers can be ready for the glorious return of our Lord and Saviour, Jesus Christ.

3.1 Strengthening Your Connection with God through Prayer and Worship

Pre-existing relationship-building theories emphasize the necessity of positive interactions for the growth and development of any relationship. However, many Christians face challenges in cultivating a vibrant and tangible relationship with God, Whom they cannot physically see or touch. Yet, their desire is not merely to believe in God, but to engage in a dynamic relationship with Him.

Ancient Bible teaching beautifully articulates that humanity's ultimate purpose is to glorify God and enjoy Him forever. This implies a deep longing to experience who God is and what He is like. To achieve this, acquiring knowledge of God becomes essential. Just as initial interactions between individuals involve asking questions to learn about each other, so too does God desire us to inquire about Him.

In contrast to human relationships, where both parties are equals, God is the great King and we are His servants. Yet, as His servants, we have the privilege of addressing Him in prayer. Prayer serves as a profound means of conversing with God, enabling us to interact with Him and deepen our understanding of His character.

Through prayer, we can seek God for help, guidance and revelation, knowing that He graciously responds to those who earnestly seek Him. Indeed, it is God Who initiates the process of finding us, exemplifying His loving and merciful nature.

As individuals persistently seek God through prayer, they inevitably gain more knowledge of Him, leading to a deeper comprehension of His character and fostering a more intimate relationship with Him. Therefore, prayer serves as the conduit through which individuals can actively engage with God, seek His presence and grow in intimacy with Him. This intimate knowledge of God not only enriches the individual's spiritual journey, but also strengthens their relationship with the Divine.

Deepening your relationship with God through prayer and worship is foundational to spiritual growth and intimacy with the Lord. Here are some practical steps to help you grow closer to God through these summarized spiritual disciplines:

Establish a Regular Prayer Routine: Set aside specific times each day to spend in prayer. Whether it's in the morning, during your lunch break or before bed, consistency is key. Find a quiet place where you can focus and communicate with God openly and honestly.

Use Various Prayer Methods: Explore different prayer methods to keep your prayer life fresh and vibrant. This could include intercessory prayer, meditation on Scripture, journaling your prayers or practicing the Lord's Prayer as a model.

Pray with Scripture: Incorporate God's Word into your prayers by reading Scripture passages and praying through them. Allow the Holy Spirit to speak to you through Scripture and guide your prayers accordingly.

Practice Listening Prayer: Cultivate a listening ear to hear God's voice in prayer. Spend time in silence and stillness, waiting on the Lord and allowing Him to speak to your heart. Be open to receiving His guidance, comfort and wisdom.

Maintain an Attitude of Gratitude: Cultivate a heart of gratitude in your prayers, thanking God for His blessings, provision and faithfulness. Gratitude fosters a spirit of humility and dependence on God, recognizing His goodness in every aspect of your life.

Engage in Worship: Worship is more than just singing songs; it's an expression of love, adoration and reverence for God. Attend corporate worship gatherings regularly, participate wholeheartedly and allow the music and lyrics to lead you into God's presence.

Sing and Make Music to the Lord: Incorporate singing and music into your personal worship times. Sing hymns, choruses or your own spontaneous songs of praise to God. Let your worship be authentic and from the heart, lifting up the name of Jesus in adoration and awe.

Practice Contemplative Worship: Set aside moments for contemplative worship where you simply dwell in God's presence without words or music. Allow yourself to rest in His love, basking in His glory and experiencing His peace that surpasses understanding.

Engage in Corporate Worship: Participate actively in your local church's worship services, fellowship and community life. Worshiping together with other believers strengthens your faith, encourages unity and fosters spiritual growth.

Seek Spiritual Mentors and Community: Surround yourself with fellow believers who can encourage, challenge and support you in your spiritual journey. Seek out mentors or spiritual directors who can provide guidance, accountability and prayer support.

The attitude of prioritizing prayer and worship in your daily life will deepen your relationship with God, draw you closer to His heart and make you experience His transforming presence in a profound and life-changing way. Allow these spiritual disciplines to shape your character, align your will with God's and empower you to live a life that glorifies Him in all you do.

3.2 Studying and Meditating on God's Word Regularly

A firm understanding of God's Word is crucial for Christians who aim to be ready, blameless and unblemished when Christ returns. Sometimes, the idea of "studying" may trigger memories of past academic struggles, leading to reluctance or hesitation in approaching this task. However, it is comforting to realize that in 2 Timothy 2:15, the word "study" actually means to "be diligent." This implies that one doesn't need extraordinary mental abilities to delve into the Bible, but rather a sincere desire to comprehend its teachings and be transformed by them. Every Christian reader should aspire to this.

Nevertheless, it's important to employ some basic methods and tools to aid in understanding God's Word. These may include utilizing resources like commentaries, concordances and dictionaries, as well as taking relevant notes on specific passages or overall themes of certain books. It's also gratifying to God when we document our reflections, emotions and prayers in response to His Word. As the Psalmist frequently expresses, cherishing God's law and meditating on it day and night should be our earnest longing (Psalms 119:11). This desire reflects our aim to internalize God's Word, relying on it during trials and allowing it to guard us against sin.

The pivotal concept here is the idea of "keeping God's words in his heart," for these very words will ultimately judge our thoughts, attitudes and actions. Therefore, our dedication to understanding and internalizing God's Word is not merely an intellectual pursuit, but a spiritual discipline with profound implications for our lives.

Studying and meditating on God's Word regularly is vital for spiritual growth, understanding His will and deepening our relationship with Him. Here are some practical steps to help you engage in this spiritual discipline:

Set Aside Dedicated Time: Schedule specific times in your day or week dedicated to studying and meditating on God's Word. Treat this time as a priority and guard it against distractions.

Choose a Quiet and Distraction-Free Environment: Find a quiet and comfortable place where you can focus without interruptions. Eliminate distractions such as electronic devices or noise that may hinder your concentration.

Start with Prayer: Begin your study time with prayer, inviting the Holy Spirit to guide you, illuminate Scripture and speak to your heart. Ask God to open your eyes and ears to understand His Word and apply it to your life.

Select a Passage or Topic: Choose a specific passage of Scripture or a topic that you feel led to explore. You can follow a structured reading plan, study a particular book of the Bible or focus on a theme relevant to your spiritual journey.

Read and Reflect: Read the selected passage carefully, paying attention to context, themes and key verses. Reflect on what the passage reveals about God, His character, His promises and His will for your life.

Ask Questions: Engage with the text by asking questions such as: What does this passage teach me about God? What is the main message or theme? How does this apply to my life? What changes do I need to make as a result of what I've learned?

Use Study Tools: Utilize study tools such as concordances, commentaries, study Bibles and online resources to deepen your understanding of Scripture. These resources can provide valuable insights, historical context and theological interpretations.

Take Notes and Journal: Keep a notebook or journal to record your thoughts, insights, prayers and reflections as you study God's Word. Writing down your observations can help reinforce your learning and provide a record of your spiritual journey.

Meditate and Memorize: Take time to meditate on key verses or passages, pondering their meaning and allowing them to sink deep into your heart. Consider memorizing Scripture to hide God's Word in your heart and apply it in your daily life (Psalms 119:11).

Apply What You Learn: The ultimate goal of studying God's Word is not just intellectual knowledge, but transformation of heart and mind. Apply the truths you've learned to your life, seeking to live in obedience to God's Word and walk in His ways.

Share with Others: Discuss your insights and discoveries with fellow believers, friends or family members. Sharing what you've learned can deepen your understanding, encourage others and foster community around God's Word.

By consistently studying and meditating on God's Word, you will grow in spiritual maturity, deepen your relationship with God and experience the transformative power of His truth in your life. Allow Scripture to be a lamp to your feet and a light to your path, guiding you in righteousness and leading you closer to the heart of God.

3.3 Living a Life of Holiness and Righteousness

The pursuit of holiness is essentially a journey toward becoming more like Christ. Jesus Christ, the only Person to ever fully please God in thought, word and deed, embodied perfect love for the Father in all He said and did. His life exemplified complete obedience to God's will and the advancement of God's Kingdom. In 1 John 2:6, John emphasizes the call for believers to walk as Christ walked, underscoring the imperative of imitating Him. This process of becoming more Christlike unfolds gradually over many years with each step drawing the believer closer to Christ while distancing them from sin and worldliness, thus progressing towards holiness.

The Hebrew word for "holy" signifies being set apart, emphasizing purity and cleanliness. In the Old Testament, it describes God Himself as designated for His people and the observance of the Sabbath. In the New Testament, holiness extends to abstaining from worldly desires and sins and a wholehearted dedication to God's ways. Peter urges believers to be holy in all aspects of life, echoing God's call to be set apart (1 Peter 1:15). Similarly, Paul identifies Christians as saints or set apart ones, urging them to separate themselves from ungodliness and impurity, aligning with God's character (2 Corinthians 6:16-18).

Although the term "holiness" may not be commonly understood in today's secular world and may even evoke notions of religious legalism, it remains foundational to Christian living. At its core, holiness signifies being set apart for God's purposes, reflecting His character and renouncing anything contrary to it. For believers, holiness isn't merely an abstract concept, but the very essence of God's transformative work in their lives, guiding them toward a life that glorifies Him.

Living a life of holiness and righteousness is central to the Christian faith and is a reflection of our relationship with God. Here are practical steps to help cultivate holiness and righteousness in your life:

Commit to God's Standards: Make a conscious decision to align your life with God's standards of holiness and righteousness as revealed in His Word. Recognize that holiness is not about religious perfection or asceticism, but about a heart set apart for God's purposes at all times (1 Peter 1:15-16).

Seek God's Will: Regularly seek God's will through prayer, seeking His guidance and direction in all areas of your life. Surrender your desires, plans and ambitions to Him, allowing His will to shape your decisions and actions (Proverbs 3:5-6).

Renew Your Mind: Transform your mind by immersing yourself in God's Word and allowing it to shape your thoughts, attitudes and beliefs (Romans 12:2). Reject worldly influences and embrace biblical truth as the standard for your life.

Practice Obedience: Obey God's commandments out of love and reverence for Him (John 14:15). Strive to obey His Word in all areas of your life, including your relationships, finances, speech and behaviour.

Confess and Repent of Sin: Regularly examine your heart and confess any sins to God. Repentance involves turning away from sin and turning toward God, seeking His forgiveness and cleansing (1 John 1:9). Allow the Holy Spirit to convict you of sin and lead you in paths of righteousness.

Guard Your Heart: Guard your heart against sinful influences and temptations that can lead you astray (Proverbs 4:23). Be mindful of the company you keep, the media you consume and the environments you expose yourself to.

Cultivate Virtues: Cultivate virtues such as love, joy, peace, patience, kindness, goodness, faithfulness, gentleness and self-control (Galatians 5:22-23). Strive to embody the character of Christ in your thoughts, words and actions.

Practice Forgiveness: Forgive those who have wronged you, releasing bitterness, resentment and anger. Follow Christ's example of forgiveness and extend grace to others as you have received grace from God (Ephesians 4:32).

Serve Others: Serve others with humility and compassion, following Christ's example of selfless love and sacrificial service (Matthew 20:28). Look for opportunities to meet the needs of others and demonstrate God's love in practical ways.

Remain Spiritually Focused: Keep your focus on spiritual growth and maturity, prioritizing your relationship with God above all else. Stay connected to the body of Christ through fellowship, worship and discipleship and surround yourself with believers who encourage and support your spiritual journey.

Persevere in Faith: Persevere in faith and endurance, knowing that the journey of holiness is a lifelong process. Trust in God's faithfulness to continue the work He has begun in you and rely on His strength to overcome obstacles and challenges along the way (Philippians 1:6).

Therefore, by pursuing holiness and righteousness in your life, you will experience the abundant life that God desires for you and become a shining light that reflects His glory to the world around you.

3.4 Spreading the Gospel and Radiating God's Love

Spreading the good news, also known as evangelism, holds profound significance in preparing for the imminent return of the Lord. To share the good news is to convey the message of Jesus Christ and His redemptive work on our behalf. Jesus entrusted His followers with the Great Commission, instructing them to make disciples of all nations, teaching obedience to His commands and assuring them of His continual presence until the end of time (Matthew 28:18-20). This monumental task, though daunting, is made achievable through the empowerment of the Holy Spirit, Whom God has promised to equip believers with for the purpose of global witness (Acts 1:8).

Effective evangelism requires a solid comprehension of the good news and its implications. Therefore, it's crucial to possess a thorough understanding of the Bible, particularly the New Testament, which elucidates the message of Jesus Christ. Practicing articulating this message to others fosters readiness to seize opportunities for sharing it. Additionally, remaining receptive to the leading of the Holy Spirit is paramount, as He guides believers in maximizing opportunities and accurately communicating the gospel message.

In essence, the spreading of the good news is not only a divine mandate, but also an integral aspect of Christian discipleship. It is through the faithful proclamation of the gospel that individuals are drawn into relationship with Christ, contributing to the fulfillment of God's redemptive plan and the anticipation of Christ's imminent return. Sharing the good news of Jesus Christ and spreading God's love is a central aspect of the Christian faith and a calling for all believers. Here are practical steps to help you effectively share the gospel and demonstrate God's love to others:

1. **Understand the Gospel**: Gain a clear understanding of the gospel message, which is the good news of salvation through Jesus Christ. Be able to articulate the key components of the gospel, including God's love for humanity, humanity's sinfulness, Jesus' sacrificial death and resurrection and the call to repentance and faith (1 Corinthians 15:1-4).

2. **Live Out Your Faith**: Let your life be a living testimony of God's love and grace. Demonstrate Christ-like character through your actions, attitudes and behaviours, reflecting His love, compassion and mercy to those around you (Matthew 5:16).

3. **Build Authentic Relationships**: Cultivate genuine relationships with others based on love, trust and respect. Take time to listen to people's stories, empathize with their struggles and show genuine

care and concern for their well-being (John 13:34-35).

4. **Pray for Opportunities**: Pray regularly for opportunities to share the gospel and demonstrate God's love to others. Ask God to open doors for conversation, to soften hearts and to prepare people to receive His truth and grace (Colossians 4:3).

5. **Be Bold and Courageous**: Step out in faith and be bold in sharing your faith with others. Don't be afraid of rejection or opposition, but trust in the power of the Holy Spirit to work through you (Acts 4:29).

6. **Share Your Story**: Share your personal testimony of how Jesus Christ has transformed your life. Be authentic and transparent about your journey of faith, highlighting God's grace, forgiveness and redemption in your life (Revelation 12:11).

7. **Use Your Gifts and Talents**: Utilize your unique gifts, talents and passions to share the gospel and serve others. Whether it's through evangelism, hospitality, acts of service or creative expression, find creative ways to communicate God's love and truth (1 Peter 4:10-11).

8. **Use Relevant Resources**: Utilize resources such as gospel tracts, books, videos or websites to share the gospel in a clear and compelling way. Be prepared to answer questions and engage in meaningful dialogue with others about their faith (1 Peter 3:15).

9. **Invite Others to Church and Community**: Invite people to church services, Bible studies, small groups or community events where they can experience God's love and hear the message of salvation. Offer a welcoming and inclusive environment where people feel accepted and valued (Hebrews 10:24-25).

10. **Follow Up and Disciple**: Follow up with individuals who have expressed interest in the gospel and provide ongoing support and discipleship. Walk alongside them in their spiritual journey, answering questions, providing encouragement and helping them grow in their relationship with Christ (Matthew 28:19-20).

11. **Trust in God's Timing and Sovereignty**: Remember that ultimately, it is God Who saves and transforms hearts. Trust in His timing and sovereignty, knowing that He is at work in the lives of those you are reaching out to, drawing them to Himself in His perfect timing (John 6:44).

The good news of Jesus Christ that you shared and spreading God's love in both word and deed play a significant role in God's Kingdom work of reconciling people to Himself and bringing hope and healing to a broken world. May your life be a shining testimony of God's love and grace, drawing others into a life-changing relationship with Jesus Christ.

3.5 Fostering Humility and a Heart of Service

Humility is an active practice rooted in self-awareness of one's limitations, accompanied by a proactive effort to overcome them, coupled with a disregard for status before both God and humanity. In contrast, the term pride carries a negative connotation, denoting an excessive belief in one's superiority, an unhealthy self-love and a boasting in things that ought to bring shame. God's favour towards the humble and His disapproval of the proud stem from ethical and spiritual distinctions.

Scripture emphasizes that one can possess low social status and still harbour sinful pride, negating the value of their gifts. Conversely, God's goodness tends to elevate and restore the humble while bringing down the prideful. An illustrative example is found in Isaiah's analogy of the potter and the clay, where God promises to expose the pride, vanity and rebellion of those who oppose His word (Jeremiah 18:9-10). Similarly, instances in Scripture depict God's favour towards the humble, often from oppressed or lowly backgrounds.

Since Satan's rebellion, his disdain for truth and humility has influenced humanity, leading many astray. Despite his own desire for these virtues, Satan consistently distorts and contradicts them. The Bible associates his influence with the downfall of numerous proud individuals who met miserable ends. Throughout history, stark contrasts have emerged between the iniquitous proud and the godly humble. Jesus himself highlighted these distinctions in His Sermon on the Mount, contrasting the humble, repentant and righteous with the proud, self-sufficient and superficially religious. Pride and humility serve as defining characteristics of these opposing groups, leading to discernible differences in their lives.

In summary, humility entails recognizing one's limitations, seeking growth and esteeming others above oneself, while pride manifests as an inflated sense of self-importance and a disregard for God and others. These contrasting attitudes have enduring consequences, shaping the paths of the righteous and the unrighteous alike. Here are practical steps to help you develop humility and embrace a servant's heart:

Study the Example of Jesus: Look to Jesus as the ultimate example of humility and servanthood (Philippians 2:5-8). Study His life, teachings and actions recorded in the Gospels and seek to emulate His humility in your own life.

Pray for Humility: Humbly acknowledge your need for God's grace and ask Him to cultivate humility in your heart. Pray for the Holy Spirit to convict you of pride and selfishness and to transform your attitude to one of humility and servanthood (James 4:10).

Examine Your Heart: Regularly examine your heart and motives, asking God to reveal areas of pride, arrogance or self-centeredness. Be willing to confess and repent of any attitudes or behaviours that are contrary to humility (Psalms 139:23-24).

Practice Self-Emptying Love: Follow Jesus' example of self-emptying love, putting the needs of others above your own (Philippians 2:3-4). Look for opportunities to serve and bless others without seeking recognition or reward.

Serve Others with Joy: Approach serving others as an opportunity to express love and gratitude to God. Serve with joy and enthusiasm, knowing that your service is ultimately unto the Lord (Colossians 3:23-24).

Be Willing to Serve in Small Ways: Embrace opportunities to serve in small, humble ways, such as washing dishes, running errands or performing acts of kindness. Recognize that no act of service is too small when done with a humble heart (Matthew 25:40).

Listen and Learn from Others: Be open to learning from others, especially those who are different from you or in positions of lesser status. Listen attentively to their perspectives, experiences and needs and seek to understand and empathize with them (James 1:19).

Accept Correction Gracefully: Receive feedback and correction from others with humility and grace. Be willing to acknowledge your mistakes and shortcomings and humbly learn from them for growth and improvement (Proverbs 12:1).

Choose Gentleness and Patience: Cultivate a spirit of gentleness and patience in your interactions with others. Avoid being easily offended or defensive and respond with grace and kindness, even in challenging situations (Ephesians 4:2-3).

Serve in Your Sphere of Influence: Serve faithfully and sacrificially in your sphere of influence, whether it's within your family, church, workplace or community. Look for ways to meet the practical needs of those around you and to be a blessing wherever you go (Galatians 6:10).

Give God the Glory: Recognize that true humility involves giving all glory and honour to God, acknowledging that any gifts, talents or opportunities for service come from Him (1 Corinthians 10:31). Point others to Jesus through your words and actions, magnifying His name above your own.

Possessing the spirit of humility and servanthood will reflect in you the character of Christ and bring glory to God in your relationships, actions and attitudes. May you find joy and fulfillment in serving others and may your life be a testament to the transforming power of humility and love.

3.6 Inspiration and Optimism Amidst the Season of Anticipation

The anticipation of the Lord's return is not a passive waiting, but an active period of preparation. While we eagerly await His coming, we trust in God's perfect timing, knowing that He is always punctual.

Though discouragement may creep in, perseverance is essential. It's easy to lose heart or become complacent, but we must remain steadfast, keeping our focus on the future reality and living each day in anticipation of the culmination of human history.

Preparing for the Lord's return involves living in a manner that reflects readiness to meet Him at any moment. This requires a commitment to righteousness and goodness, even when it's difficult or unpopular. While waiting, it is natural to experience a mix of tension, hope and fear. However, we are encouraged to replace fear and anxiety with hope and joy, as we trust in the loving nature of God. Our hope isn't mere wishful thinking, but a confident expectation based on God's faithfulness in fulfilling His promises.

Our ultimate hope lies in the return of our Lord Jesus Christ and this hope profoundly impacts how we live in the present. It motivates us to live faithfully and obediently, knowing that our actions today are in preparation for His glorious return.

Therefore, as we eagerly await His coming, let us be found vigilant, joyfully anticipating the fulfillment of God's plan and the ultimate restoration of all things. In times of waiting, it is natural to feel impatient, discouraged or uncertain about the future. However, as Christians, we have a source of encouragement and hope that sustains us through every season of waiting. Here are some key truths to hold onto during times of waiting:

Trust in God's Timing: Remember that God's timing is perfect, even when it doesn't align with our own plans or expectations (Ecclesiastes 3:1). Trust that He knows what is best for you and that He is working all things together for your good, according to His purpose (Romans 8:28).

Lean on God's Promises: Find comfort and strength in God's promises, knowing that He is faithful to fulfill His word (2 Corinthians 1:20). Claim promises such as Jeremiah 29:11 assures us of God's plans to prosper us and give us hope and a future.

Draw Near to God in Prayer: Use this season of waiting as an opportunity to draw near to God in prayer. Pour out your heart to Him, expressing your hopes, fears and frustrations. Seek His guidance, wisdom and peace as you wait on Him (Philippians 4:6-7).

Find Strength in Scripture: Spend time meditating on Scripture and allowing God's Word to speak to your heart. Find encouragement in passages such as Isaiah 40:31 which promises that those who wait on the Lord will renew their strength.

Remember God's Faithfulness: Reflect on past experiences of God's faithfulness in your life. Recall moments when He provided, protected and answered prayers in ways you never expected. Let these memories strengthen your faith and trust in Him (Lamentations 3:22-23).

Seek Fellowship and Support: Surround yourself with fellow believers who can offer encouragement, support and prayer during your time of waiting. Share your burdens with trusted friends or mentors who can walk alongside you and lift you up in times of need (Galatians 6:2).

Focus on Growth and Preparation: Use this season of waiting as an opportunity for growth and preparation. Ask God to reveal areas of your life where He desires to refine you and shape you more into His likeness. Seek to deepen your relationship with Him and grow in spiritual maturity (James 1:2-4).

Practice Patience and Perseverance: Cultivate patience and perseverance as you wait for God's timing to unfold. Remember that waiting is an essential part of the Christian journey and that God is using this time to prepare you for what lies ahead (Hebrews 10:36).

Serve and Bless Others: Look for opportunities to serve and bless others while you wait. Keep your focus outward, seeking to be a source of encouragement and hope to those around you. God can use your acts of kindness to bring light into someone else's darkness (Matthew 5:16).

Hold onto Hope: Anchor your soul in the hope of God's promises, knowing that He is faithful and trustworthy. Keep your eyes fixed on Jesus, the Author and Perfecter of our faith, Who endured the cross for the joy set before Him (Hebrews 12:2).

As you navigate the season of waiting, may you find encouragement and hope in God's presence, His promises and His unfailing love.

Trust that He is with you every step of the way, guiding you, sustaining you and leading you into His perfect plan for your life.

4

DISCOVERING RESILIENCE AND SOLACE IN THE ASSURANCES OF GOD

GOD'S faithfulness is a source of strength and comfort for believers. We can place our complete trust in Him because His promises are the cornerstones of Christian living. Throughout the Bible, God assures us of His help in every circumstance. By meditating on these promises, our faith is strengthened. It's crucial to heed God's commands and rely on His assistance to fulfill them. When we are obedient and do our part, God faithfully fulfills His promises, often exceeding our expectations.

In times of doubt and temptation, we can combat Satan's lies with the truth of God's promises. Just as Jesus did in the wilderness, we can use the Word of God as a powerful weapon in spiritual warfare. God's promises serve as guiding lights in areas of uncertainty or difficulty. When faced with indecision, we can search for a promise relevant to our situation and trust that God will lead us along the right path, as He has promised.

Therefore, let us anchor our faith in the unshakeable truth of God's promises. By clinging to His faithful assurances and relying on His help, we navigate life's challenges with confidence and assurance, knowing that God is always true to His word.

Finding strength and comfort in God's promises is essential for navigating life's challenges and uncertainties. Here are some key ways to draw strength and comfort from God's promises:

Identify Promises in Scripture: Take time to search the Bible for promises that speak to your specific needs and circumstances. Promises related to peace, provision, guidance, protection and strength are especially comforting during difficult times.

Meditate on God's Word: Set aside regular time to meditate on Scripture and reflect on the promises of God. Allow His Word to penetrate your heart and mind, bringing comfort, encouragement and hope (Psalms 119:105).

Claim Promises in Prayer: Bring God's promises before Him in prayer, affirming your belief in His faithfulness and asking Him to fulfill His word in your life. Pray with confidence, knowing that God hears and answers the prayers of His children (1 John 5:14-15).

Memorize Scripture: Commit key promises to memory so that you can recall them in times of need. Having God's Word stored in your heart enables you to draw upon His promises for strength and encouragement whenever you face challenges (Psalms 119:11).

Anchor Your Faith in God's Character: Trust in the character of God as the foundation for His promises. Remember that He is faithful, loving, compassionate and trustworthy, and His promises are sure because of Who He is (2 Corinthians 1:20).

Look to Jesus as the Fulfillment of Promises: Recognize that Jesus Christ is the ultimate fulfillment of God's promises. Find assurance and hope in His life, death and resurrection, knowing that through Him, all of God's promises are "Yes" and "Amen" (2 Corinthians 1:20).

Testify to God's Faithfulness: Share stories of God's faithfulness and the fulfillment of His promises in your life with others. Testify to His goodness and grace, encouraging others to trust in His promises and experience His faithfulness for themselves (Psalms 107:2).

Encourage Others with Promises: Use God's promises to encourage and uplift others who are facing difficulties or struggles. Share relevant Scripture verses with them, praying that God's promises will bring them comfort, strength and hope in their time of need (1 Thessalonians 5:11).

Persist in Faith and Trust: Hold onto God's promises with unwavering faith and trust, even when circumstances seem bleak or uncertain. Choose to believe His Word above your feelings or circumstances, knowing that He is able to do immeasurably more than all we ask or imagine (Ephesians 3:20).

Give Thanks for Promises Fulfilled: Express gratitude to God for His faithfulness in fulfilling His promises. Celebrate answered prayers and testimonies of God's provision, protection, guidance and blessings, giving Him glory and honour for His goodness (Psalms 103:2).

When your anchor of faith holds in God's promises, you can find strength, comfort and hope to persevere through life's trials and challenges. Trust in His unfailing word, knowing that He is faithful to fulfill all that He has promised and rest in the assurance of His love and care for you.

4.2 Trusting in God's Perfect Timing

In the New Testament, James 5:8 encourages Christians to embody patience in all aspects of life. *"Be ye also patient; stablish your hearts: for the coming of the Lord draweth nigh."* Drawing from the analogy of a farmer awaiting the rains for his crops, James underscores the necessity of enduring patiently through trials and tribulations without wavering in faith.

He emphasizes the imminent return of the Lord as a motivating factor for perseverance, keeping hope alive and providing encouragement during challenging times. Similarly, Peter emphasizes that the Christian's hope in God's promises, including the promise of Christ's return, enables steadfastness in the face of adversity.

Numerous biblical examples illustrate the consequences of failing to wait on the Lord. Abraham, for instance, impatiently sought to fulfill God's promise of a son by taking matters into his own hands, resulting in the birth of Ishmael and subsequent conflicts. The Israelites similarly faltered in their faith, resorting to idolatry while waiting for Moses to return from Mount Sinai. These instances highlight the dangers of doubt and impatience, often leading to detrimental outcomes.

Conversely, waiting on the Lord yields blessings. David's journey to kingship exemplifies this as he patiently trusted in God's timing despite facing numerous challenges. His steadfast faith is beautifully expressed in Psalms 62:1-2, affirming God as his salvation and fortress. The Christian journey inherently involves waiting and learning to trust in God's perfect timing.

In Hebrew, the word for trust is synonymous with waiting, emphasizing the inseparable connection between the two. True trust in God entails contentment in waiting for His will to unfold. Thus, any reluctance to wait on God reflects a lack of trust in Him. The Christian life is characterized by a steadfast reliance on God's timing, with waiting serving as a testament to our unwavering faith in Him.

Trusting in God's perfect timing can be challenging, especially when we are eager for things to happen according to our own schedules. However, understanding and embracing God's timing is crucial for our faith journey. Here are some key principles to help us trust in God's perfect timing:

Recognize God's Sovereignty: Remember that God is sovereign over all things, including time itself. He sees the bigger picture and knows what is best for us (Isaiah 55:8-9). Trusting in His sovereignty means surrendering our own plans and agendas to His greater purpose.

Acknowledge His Wisdom: Trust that God's timing is based on His infinite wisdom and understanding. He knows the beginning from the end and orchestrates events in accordance with His perfect plan (Job 12:13).

Wait with Patience: Develop patience as you wait for God's timing to unfold. Understand that waiting is an essential part of the Christian journey and that God often uses times of waiting to refine our character, deepen our faith and prepare us for His blessings (Psalms 27:14).

Believe in His Faithfulness: Remind yourself of God's faithfulness throughout history and in your own life. Reflect on past experiences where God has come through for you in unexpected ways or at just the right moment.

82

Trust that He will continue to be faithful in the future (Lamentations 3:22-23).

Seek His Guidance: Stay connected to God through prayer and seek His guidance in all things. Ask Him to reveal His timing and direction for your life and be willing to follow His lead, even when it doesn't align with your own plans (Proverbs 3:5-6).

Find Peace in His Presence: Rest in the assurance of God's presence with you as you wait. Draw near to Him in times of uncertainty and find peace in His steadfast love and unwavering faithfulness (Psalms 46:10).

Trust His Provision: Trust that God will provide for your needs according to His timing. Have confidence that He knows what you need before you even ask and that He will supply all your needs according to His riches in glory (Matthew 6:8; Philippians 4:19).

Stay Focused on Him: Keep your focus on God rather than on the timing of His answers or blessings. Seek to deepen your relationship with Him, grow in intimacy with Him and align your desires with His will (Colossians 3:1-2).

Celebrate His Timing: When God's timing does manifest in your life, celebrate and give thanks for His faithfulness. Recognize His hand at work and testify to His goodness, both to yourself and to others (Psalms 40:5).

Encourage Others: Use your experiences of trusting in God's timing to encourage and support others who may be struggling with waiting. Share stories of God's faithfulness and remind them that He is trustworthy and reliable (1 Thessalonians 5:11).

Trusting in God's perfect timing requires faith, patience and surrender. As we learn to trust in Him more deeply, we can rest assured that His timing is always perfect and His plans for us are good, pleasing and perfect (Romans 8:28).

4.3 Persevering in Faith during Trials and Tribulations

Perseverance during trials and tribulations is intrinsically linked to trusting in God's perfect timing. These challenges often test our faith to its limits, leading us to question whether God truly remains in control. Understanding why God permits trials and tribulations in our lives is crucial for enduring them with our faith intact. These trials serve as refining processes for our faith, much like gold is purified in fire and emerges more precious than before.

When our faith endures trials, it demonstrates its genuineness and surpasses the value of gold. As stated in 1 Peter 1:7, genuine faith, proven through trials, is of greater worth than gold refined by fire. This understanding can provide encouragement and motivation to persevere through hardships.

Jeremiah exemplifies this kind of persevering faith when he acknowledges God's testing of his attitude (Jeremiah 12:3). Despite his initial complaints and questions, Jeremiah persists in his faith and continues to serve God. Eventually, he gains a deeper understanding of God's justice. This illustrates that by persevering through trials with the correct understanding of God's purpose and faith in His faithfulness, we can maintain our faith even in the midst of adversity.

Therefore, recognizing that God uses trials to refine our faith and believing that He will see us through them enables us to endure with hope and confidence. With this perspective, we can emerge from trials strengthened in faith and closer to understanding the depth of God's love and sovereignty.

Persevering in faith during trials and tribulations is a profound testament to the strength and resilience of the human spirit. In the face of adversity, whether personal, societal, or existential, faith serves as an anchor, grounding individuals in hope, courage and conviction.

Throughout history, countless individuals have drawn upon their faith as a source of sustenance and solace during times of trial. Whether grappling with illness, loss, injustice or upheaval, the unwavering belief in a higher power or greater purpose can imbue even the darkest moments with meaning and purpose.

At the heart of perseverance in faith lies an unyielding trust in God's providence. It is a steadfast commitment to surrendering to the inherent mystery of life, embracing both its joys and sorrows with equanimity and grace. In the crucible of adversity, faith becomes a transformative force, forging resilience, character and spiritual depth.

Moreover, perseverance in faith fosters a sense of interconnectedness and solidarity with fellow travelers on the journey of life. It inspires acts of compassion, generosity and service, as individuals extend a hand of support to those navigating their own trials and tribulations. In this way, faith becomes a catalyst for collective healing and transformation, binding communities together in a shared quest for redemption and renewal.

Yet, the path of perseverance in faith is not devoid of challenges or doubts. It demands courage to confront the existential questions that arise in the midst of suffering and uncertainty. It requires humility to embrace the limitations of human understanding and to hold space for ambiguity and paradox. Also, it calls for resilience to weather the storms of doubt and despair that may assail the soul along the way.

In the end, the journey of persevering in faith during trials and tribulations is a testament to the indomitable spirit of the human soul. It is a journey of awakening to the inherent resilience, wisdom and grace that reside within each individual, waiting to be uncovered and embraced. It is a journey of deepening trust in the unseen forces that guide and sustain us, even in the darkest of times.

In the end, perseverance in faith is not merely about enduring hardship, but about transmuting suffering into wisdom, fear into courage and despair into hope. It is a sacred pilgrimage of the heart, leading us ever closer to the divine source of love and light that shines eternally within us and around us, illuminating the path towards wholeness and redemption.

4.4 Embracing Anticipation and Joy for the Coming of the Lord

The anticipation of Christ's return, as emphasized in Titus 2:13; Hebrews 9:28 and Revelation 22:20, profoundly shapes the Christian's outlook and lifestyle. Just as the awareness of impending death alters one's perspective on life, so does the anticipation of Christ's return transform how believers live. Christians are called to live in readiness for Christ's imminent return, eagerly awaiting His arrival and striving to hear the commendation, "Well done, good and faithful servant."

This eager expectation infuses believers with joy even amidst trials and suffering, as they recognize these hardships as temporary and light compared to the eternal glory awaiting them when Christ appears. This perspective, rooted in passages like Romans 8:18; 2 Corinthians 4:16-18; 1 Thessalonians 4:13-18 and 1 Peter 1:3-9, enables believers to endure with hope and confidence, knowing that their present sufferings will be surpassed by the eternal weight of glory to come.

Transitioning to the Gospel According to Mark, the author's opening proclamation in Mark 1:1 sets the tone for his narrative, presenting Jesus Christ as the Son of God and the Bearer of the good news. Mark's gospel unveils the journey of John Mark, intricately woven with the early workings of the Church. Despite initial setbacks, Mark's journey reflects redemption and growth, mirroring the transformative power of Christ's love.

Mark's gospel emphasizes Christ's ministry, servanthood, and sacrificial death, inviting readers to ponder the profound mystery of Christ's incarnation. As readers journey through Mark's narrative, they encounter the transformative power of Christ's love, the radical nature of His Kingdom and the call to discipleship.

In essence, both the anticipation of Christ's return and the proclamation of the Gospel According to Mark underscore the centrality of Christ in the Christian faith. Anticipating His return shapes believers' lives, while Mark's gospel invites readers to encounter the living Christ and be transformed by His presence. Together, these aspects illuminate the essence of the Christian journey and the hope found in the good news of Jesus Christ.

Therefore, living with anticipation and joy for the Lord's return is a profound expression of faith and hope for believers in Christian journey on earth. It encompasses a state of readiness and expectation for the promised return of Jesus Christ, as foretold in Scriptures.

Central to this anticipation is a deep-seated conviction in the fulfillment of divine promises and the realization of God's Kingdom on Earth. It is rooted in the belief that Christ will return in glory to establish a reign of peace, justice and righteousness for all creation.

Living with anticipation and joy for the Lord's return entails an active engagement with the present moment, infused with hope for the future. It involves cultivating a sense of spiritual attentiveness and readiness, remaining vigilant and prepared for the day of Christ's coming.

At its core, this anticipation is marked by a joyful expectation of reunion with the Lord, as well as with departed loved ones who share in the hope of resurrection and eternal life. It is a source of comfort and assurance amidst life's trials and tribulations, knowing that ultimate victory over sin, suffering and death is assured through Christ's triumph. Moreover, living with anticipation and joy for the Lord's return impels believers to live lives of holiness, integrity and service. It inspires acts of compassion, justice and reconciliation, as individuals strive to embody the values of God's Kingdom here and now.

Yet, this anticipation is not passive or escapist in nature. Rather, it motivates believers to actively participate in

God's redemptive work in the world, bearing witness to the transformative power of Christ's love and grace.

In essence, living with anticipation and joy for the Lord's return is a dynamic expression of faith, hope and love. It calls believers to embrace the present with purpose and meaning, while eagerly anticipating the glorious future that awaits in the fulfillment of God's promises. It is a sacred journey of anticipation, hope and joyful expectation as believers await the day when Christ will come again to make all things new.

Mark's gospel was penned after the death of Christ, yet its inspired purpose and significance reverberate through the ages:

To Proclaim the Sonship of Christ: Mark seeks to fulfill the Old Testament prophecy of the coming Son of God by presenting Jesus to the world as the long-awaited Messiah, the Son of God incarnate (Luke 1:35).

To Pronounce the Seal of Heaven upon Christ: Mark emphasizes that Jesus bears the divine seal of approval and appointment from the Heavenly Father, declaring Him to be the Very Beloved Son of God, the King of kings (John 6:27).

To Publish the Salvation from Christ: The Gospel of Mark proclaims and heralds the salvation that comes through Christ alone, reconciling humanity with God, breaking the chains of sin and preparing souls for eternity with God (Acts 4:12).

To Portray the Supremacy of Christ: In depicting Christ's death and resurrection, Mark unveils the unparalleled greatness and supremacy of Jesus above all others in history, possessing supernatural power beyond comprehension (Mark 15:37-39).

To Prove the Servanthood of Christ: Mark reveals the paradox of Christ's divinity and servanthood, showcasing His willingness to humble Himself and serve humanity sacrificially, ultimately giving His life as a ransom for many (Philippians 2:6-8).

To Present the Sacrifice of Christ: Mark underscores the sacrificial nature of Christ's mission, highlighting His ultimate act of love and redemption by the shedding of His blood for the forgiveness of sins (Mark 10:45; 1 Corinthians 5:7).

To Preview the Second Coming of Christ: As Mark recounts the earthly ministry of Jesus, he also directs our attention to His anticipated return as the triumphant King of kings and Lord of lords, urging believers to await His coming with eager anticipation and preparedness (2 Peter 1:17, 16).

The Gospel According to Mark isn't merely a historical narrative; it's a transformative message that continues to impact lives and shape destinies. Let us embrace its call to embrace the good news of Jesus Christ, walk in His footsteps, and eagerly anticipate His return with hearts ablaze with faith and hope.

In Mark 1:2-6, we witness the fulfillment of ancient prophecies heralding the arrival of the Messiah. Centuries before Christ's birth, Isaiah and Malachi prophesied of a messenger who would prepare the way for the Lord, calling for repentance and the straightening of paths for His arrival. John the Baptist emerges as the fulfillment of these prophecies, appointed as the forerunner of Christ, tasked with preparing hearts for the imminent arrival of the Son of God.

Clad in humility and sustained by a simple diet, John embarked on his divine mission in the wilderness, proclaiming a baptism of repentance for the forgiveness of sins. His message resonated with people from all walks of life, drawing crowds from across Judea and Jerusalem to the banks of the Jordan River.

He emphasized repentance, faith in Christ, salvation and the transformative power of Christ to cleanse and sanctify hearts. John also highlighted the exalted status and supreme authority of Christ, declaring Him above all prophets and worthy of utmost reverence and obedience. He warned of impending judgment and the urgency of embracing salvation before it was too late.

John's persuasive preaching and humble demeanour left a profound impact, prompting many to confess their sins and be baptized.

Reflecting on John the Baptist's ministry, we are reminded of our own calling to proclaim the gospel with conviction and humility, urging others to repentance and faith in Christ. Just as John prepared the way for the Lord's first coming, we are called to prepare hearts for His return.

Let us be faithful heralds of the gospel, declaring with boldness and sincerity, the good news of salvation through Jesus Christ.

Finally, brethren, always remember the verses of the Scripture written by 2 Peter 1:1-11; *"Wherefore the rather, brethren, give diligence to make your calling and election sure: for if ye do these things, ye shall never fall: For so an entrance shall be ministered unto you abundantly into the everlasting kingdom of our Lord and Saviour Jesus Christ."*

Here, Apostle Peter is telling us telling us that, there's consequence if we fall. May our decision ever be: *"For ye have need of patience, that, after ye have done the will of God, ye might receive the promise. For yet a little while, and he that shall come will come, and will not tarry. Now the just shall live by faith: but if any man draw back, my soul shall have no pleasure in him. But we are not of them who draw back unto perdition; but of them that believe to the saving of the soul"* (Hebrews 10:36-39).

May we never fall nor falter and our lives shall continually reflect the transformative power of His grace, drawing others into the Kingdom of God and paving the way for His glorious return in Jesus' name. Amen!

EPILOGUE

As we come to the conclusion of "Prepare to Meet Your Lord," we find ourselves at a sacred juncture – the end of one journey and the beginning of another. Throughout the pages of this book, we have traversed the landscapes of faith, explored the depths of spirituality and delved into the mysteries of divine encounter.

We have grappled with the questions of existence, sought the truths of eternity, and journeyed inward to the depths of our souls, but the journey does not end here. In fact, it is only just beginning. For the call to "Prepare to Meet Your Lord" is not a one-time summons, but a lifelong pursuit – a continuous striving towards greater intimacy with the Divine, deeper understanding of His will and fuller embodiment of His love.

As we reflect on the journey we have undertaken, let us remember that preparation is not a passive endeavour, but an active engagement of heart, mind and soul. It is a daily practice of prayer, meditation and self-examination.

It is a commitment to living with integrity, compassion and humility. It is a willingness to surrender our will to the will of the Divine Lord Jesus and to walk in obedience to His commandments.

As we prepare to meet our Lord, let us hold fast to the promises of His Word, the assurances of His presence and the hope of His coming. Let us stand firm in the knowledge that He Who has called us is faithful and He will bring to completion the good work He has begun in us.

So, as we bid farewell to these pages, let us go forth with hearts ablaze with faith, minds illumined with truth and spirits enlivened with hope. Let us walk boldly in the path of righteousness, trusting in the guidance of the Holy Spirit and the grace of our Lord Jesus Christ. For in the end, it is not the words we have read or the knowledge we have gained that will prepare us to meet our Lord, but the transformation of our hearts and lives by His love. May we be found faithful, may we be found ready and may we be found rejoicing in the presence of our Lord for all eternity.

In faith and anticipation,

Akinbowale Isaac Adewumi
akindewum@gmail.com

OTHER BOOKS WRITTEN BY THE SAME AUTHOR

1. Satanic Attacks and the Way Out.

2. Victorious Christian Living Essentials.

3. Prevailing Prayers of Intercession and Supplication Guides.

4. Satanic Attacks and the Way Out (Second Edition).

5. Principles of Christian Marriage and Family Life.

6. Evangelization and Christian Development.

7. Winning the Invisible War with Christ.

8. Called to be a Soldier.

9. End Time Events.

10. Christ-Centered Parenting.

11. Weeds Among the Wheat.

12. Church in the House.

References

Garza K, Goble C, Brooke J, Jay C. Framing the community data system interface. Proceedings of the 2015 British HCI Conference 2015.

https://christinprophecy.org/articles/recognizing-signs-of-the-times/

https://www.bibleinfo.com/en/topics/signs-times

www.ingramcontent.com/pod-product-compliance
Lightning Source LLC
Chambersburg PA
CBHW032146040426
42449CB00005B/421